RICHARD LEE GRANVOLD

OF TIME AND ANGELS

North Orchard Press, LLC

Cover Art by Richard Lee Granvold

Cover Design by Sean Hanson

Published by North Orchard Press, LLC

www.northorchardpress.com

ISBN: 978-1-7363148-2-1

For family and friends all.
For everybody, everywhere.
Peace and love, ever and always.

A special thanks to Sean Hanson, the Editor-in-Chief of North Orchard Press, for giving me the opportunity to have these poems published.

—The Author

Introduction

This is what the poet says;
We are true messages.
We are poems of the Living Expression,
All life is,
For all were created by the Word,
The Word, whose every Word is a true message.
I offer you, dear reader,
My true messages, my words, my poems,
Of the secrets of time and the angels,
From the year of viral variations.

Richard L. Granvold
- 2021 -

Of Time and Angels

Prologue

I offer you these poetic alliterations,
For your careful considerations,
My word blossoms are
Eddies of wind,
A map etched on stone,
White mushrooms scattered like buttons on grass,
Broken blocks of concrete on sidewalk,
Wild rabbits running to hide,
Art of snail trail drawn in slime,
Catchers of the sun.

Consider them,
With careful consideration,
With insightful insights,
My word blossoms,
Of poetic alliterations.

1 - My Lost Child

Look homeward my lost angel,
Look homeward my lost child,
Look past all the confusion,
Look past all the crowd.

Look at the ones you're passing,
Look at the homeless son,
Look at his little sister,
His little tagalong.

For I know you are looking,
As I know you often do,
Looking for a place called home,
Looking like the fool.

Look homeward my lost angel,
Look homeward my lost child,
Look homeward to a place,
You know that can't be found.

For, I say to you my lost angel,
Yes, I say to you my lost child,
Look homeward my lost angel,
To where I'm waiting for you,
And return my lost child.

2 - Moon-rose

Where the moon-rose grows,
By the broken lake,
There is a scattering of seeds that jungled, grow or die,
As all life must do.

Is this as far as you can grow moon-rose?
For you are a living time machine, all life is.
Can you make the crossing and return moon-rose,
Telling stories of the stars?

At the star-flaked rim beyond Andromeda,
Sitting at the edge where the world-winds blow,
There is all the night of the universe to explore,
Across bridges that are dragons' backs.

You whistle and listen to know where to grow.
Oh, moon-rose if you have all the universe to grow,
You can find anything, everything,
Yet tears, like stars that are circles of silver dropping from the
 sky,
Are the water that makes you grow,
So you stay close by.

3 - Like Angels on High

An angel sits in my shoulder,
Where Orion rides high over me at night,
Where the stars are bright,
In His constellation.

Bright as the eyes of the Hunter I have become,
Now that I am out and alone,
Shut out in the night,
Of His bright constellation.

And though the middle of winter,
Has set its night upon me,
In the new year of the bright Hunter,
I have become,
Somewhere, somehow, lost under the sun.

Lost and exiled from the lies,
As the old year dies,
And I turn to simpler time and things,
And talk about truth once more.

Where I have come down to the shore,
In the middle of winter,
To think of time and tides,
And stars, bright over my shoulder,
Like angels on high.

4 - Colors of Time

I see the colors of time,
Where under the trees,
In the night, fireflies gather,
Dancing like tiny jars of light,
That I may juggle into patterns of time.

Time, I see by the clock,
Is not a number to be pointed at upon the wall,
Its secret is hidden in the shadows of sundials,
That fail at night,
Where there is no light, no time,
Other than stars revolving,
And life evolving,
To some unknown end.

Even the moon is hidden soon in shadow,
Its time frozen like an ageless glacier.
Shall I be here long,
Where the night holds me still and breathless,
As the cold shadows rise,
And the glacier of the moon hangs low in the sky?

5 - Songs I Hear

The songs I hear,
When I juggle my musical spheres,
Echo in time...
Echo in time...

The stars at night,
Are equally bright,
As my jars of colored lights,
That in gentle arcs of flight,
I juggle into patterns so fair and so fine,
That delight my mind,
These fractals of time.

My mad eye has seen,
Far into the infrared,
To glimpse shadows of time travelers,
Like lost souls of the dead,
They pass us by as unseen seeds of light,
They travel,
To a dark shadow of a night,
Empty of all stars.

6 - Dubious Land

In the heart of the dubious land
Below incurious stars, lost in mist,
By the crack of the world,
Under the shelter of canopy trees,
Dwells the Heart of Time,
That even the wiser tries to hide,
From the clocks of man.
I hear time reverberating in its black abyss,
That barrier of time I cannot pass.

Like the simple, necessary prayer,
Is my clock I hold in hand,
That watch, bought in the City at World's End,
Its geared teeth chattering in the chasm.
The bright side of the sundial knows no time,
Only its fidget,
Dark shadow has the knowledge,
Necessary for me to know the time,
And not illuminated, I cannot see it.

So I listen for the bells of the tower clock,
To tell me the time of my return,

For I would go home,
Home, beyond the Forest Impassible.

I hang my head into the black abyss,
Listening for the time unknown to the Children of Wonder,
In the endless forest, far from the tower of time,
And faint, as a mere whisper, it comes,
To awaken me from this dream and its fantasy time.

7 - Who Angels Follow

Will the Angels follow me,
Like they do O-Ben,
That prophet of the poor,
Will they follow me,
As I go out the door?

Are they far,
Or are they near,
What are the voices I hear,
So fine, and so pure,
That I could see,
It is they,
Who are calling me?

O-Ben was ahead,
Ahead of them all,
The Angels were heeding,
His clarion call,
That prophet of the poor,
Ran all the way to Babylon,
That lost city of old.

Where there is a rising of the Angels,
And a rising of the poor,
A rising to God,
To uncover His secrets,
That lead one to another.
With a unity of language,
All could understand,
I built the Tower of Babel again.
That is the poet's job.

8 - Thomas Timekeeper

Thomas Timekeeper kept time for his friends,
Precious though it was,
He gathered time for Clock-man,
Builder of the fractal clock.

Clock-man lives in the Land Where Nobody Goes,
Across Dragon's Back Bridge,
That changes when the dragon rolls,
In his sleep, across that chasm,
Of time so deep.

Time slows down,
In the Land Where Nobody Goes,
There is no crowd there,
So there is room to slow the rate of time passing,
And make it everlasting,
So Clock-man will never die.

Thomas Timekeeper kept time for his friends,
A task he thought would never end,
For Clock-man had his clock,
With its never ending tick and tock,

That echoes across that chasm,
Ever resounding, never ending,
Echoing alone from across that chasm.

9 - Clock-man

Clock-man counted the hours,
Of his binary flowers,
With a digital clock,
Waiting for them to bloom,
By Blueberry Bay.
Near the shore,
He played a quiet tune,
And sang with his mandolin,
Under the Flower moon,
Of May.

Clock-man played before the waters,
Counting time with his water clock,
And thought about it for hours and hours.
Then he walked across the briny sea,
To count all the starfish below,
It was something he had to know.
Till finally he was granted his wish,
To see the dance of the starfish,
And oh, how it delighted him so,
To watch how they did go,
To and fro,

With him atop the briny sea.

And when this was read,
The little one looked up and said,
"I like that one, papa,
Read it again".

10 - Angel in the Frosted Forest

Cold,
The world has grown so cold,
All the forests are frosted,
None are left there to roam,
Except one alone.

White she is,
Whiter than the snow,
There she is,
Where the winter blossoms grow,
On whose petals she nibbles.

For what else is there to eat,
Beneath the bitter winter,
But those special blooms,
The petals of winter's flower?

This is a winter that will never end,
She will never see spring again,
Man's careless solution,
Left too much pollution.

White deer,
Last of its kind,
There are no other animals,
Left to find,
Upon all the Earth.

Alone,
The world has grown so cold,
The White Deer listens for another,
Listens for another angel,
In the frosted forest,
Until the end of time.

11 - Rain Is When the Angels Cry in Heaven

Remember Noah?
I do,
He was a friend of mine,
Noah new how much,
I cared for animals,
That is why he cared for me.

The Angels,
They began a-crying,
For the the evil raging,
Seen on the planes below.

The Angels were always watching,
For Angels are the watchers,
Of those put in their care,
Upon the hills below.

But their tears were too many,
Upon the land of plenty,
With the Golden Honey,
Of the promised land,
And so the Flood began.

12 - My Little Demon

Time's Devil,
Rolled on my table,
Then off, onto the floor,
There it stayed awhile,
Grinning with that evil smile,
Like my little demon.

My little demon is not so bad,
In fact his case is quite sad,
For he wouldn't be doing what he is doing,
If he had any choice about it.

It was an innocent thing,
What he made me do,
It hurt no one,
Not me, nor you.

In truth,
I quite wanted it,
When I first came upon it,
Oh, how it excited me so,
So I let it grow.

Yes, it is still with me,
After all these years,
Of this I want to be clear,
It is quite harmless,
If but a little queer,

Like these last, strange days,
Which have arrived here,
When none knew,
It would be like this,
It is but a final kiss,
Upon our foreheads.

13 - Dancing

Dancing on a pinhead,
I've been there before,
Spinning atop that head so small,
With a myriad of Angels,
So brave and so tall.

Dancing that war dance,
That those Angels do,
When warring against the Demons,
Fighting for me and you.

Their King is calling out,
The dancing tune,
"Get ready for the Final Battle,
Be brave and be True,
I will lead you.
None of them can stand before Me,
Yes it is true,
I have already won the Final Battle,
Upon that Cross,
Long ago."

14 - The Oak of Abraham

Come, gather under the Oak of Abraham,
Three angels will be there,
The leaves have not yet fallen,
So there is rest in its shade,
From the desert heat.

Come, gather under the Oak of Abraham,
I will give you water to drink,
I will wash your dusty feet,
Give you food to eat,
Anoint your head with olive oil,
Dress you in my robe.

Where are you going, angels?
Tell me, for I would know.

Come, gather under the Oak of Abraham,
You from Sodom,
And Gomorrah too,
Let's throw a party instead,
For I would save you,
From the destruction,

Headed your way.

Come, gather under the Oak of Abraham,
We can watch it raining destruction,
Upon the evil,
He cannot tolerate,
We will celebrate,
Brimstone and fire,
Like fireworks,
On the Fourth of July.

15 - I Killed Time

I killed time,
I didn't mean to do it,
But the situation came along,
So I took it.

I was trying,
To set back my clock,
Reverse its Tick and its Tock,
For you see,
Younger I would be.

I am old,
I should be so bold,
As to not die.

My clock got,
All un-wound up,
Too loose,
I broke its second gear.

Now I am stuck,
Frozen in time,
Neither young,
Nor too old to die.

16 - Time's Umbra

Below the forest canopy,
Ancient trees, oldest of trees,
Whose shade is an umbra of time,
Come to cover me.

Old now, here it is,
Whose shadows hold on to the past,
Clinging to it, not willing to let it go,
Time's Umbra holds the memories of the forest,
Memories which are the life of the forest,
That once existed,
And still exists in the forest today,
Under the canopy.

My umbrage was lost,
I dropped it on the wooded trail,
Of my life's forest,
It is just as well,
For I have grown,
Such as not to need it,
Or to take it,
With me, wherever I go.

I hide my memories in the forest,
To protect them for those,
Who would rob and steal,
For the sake of their own umbrage.

Time's Umbra hides them perfectly,
None shall find them,
Except for perhaps the trees,
Those time-worn,
Elders of the all-greens.

I am well satisfied,
Where it is forest quiet,
Every sound a hushed whisper,
There is beauty in the silence,
A quieting of my soul,
I know now,
All is well,
All is well, with my soul.

17 - In Moody Fog

Time's moody fog is in my mind...
In moody fog,
How long a second is depends,
On how I set my Watch,
In fogs of time.

In mists of time,
My watch is set for cold,
For cold is the mist,
Of moody fog.

In rains of time,
My watch is set for droplets,
That quench my watch,
In moody fog.

In snows of time,
I set my watch for whiteness,
Its brightness,
To burn away,
Moody fog.

In suns of time,
In time of suns,
Delight I find,
In my mind,
I set my watch to freedom,
Being set free,
That sets free my being,
Of moody fog.

18 - Obadiah Evermore

Obadiah Evermore,
Rang his bells,
Lighted his bells,
Shining with reverberating light.

Ringing in the light,
A vibration glowing,
Glowing with sound,
Whose sight delights,
With sounds not seen before,
And colors not heard before.

Obadiah strikes his light-bell,
With a lightning hammer,
Spark spears shooting off,
To the intended target,
A black hole bull's eye.

On the other side,
Of bull's eye black hole,
Sun-Catcher, Light-Changer,
Heard a ringing of bells,

Spiritual bells, sanctuary bells,
A ship's bell ringing for boarding,
Ringing for last call,
Reverberating an angel's light,
Shining from the other side.

Angel bells of heaven,
Obadiah Evermore's bells of light,
Are lighted and ringing,
By the Throne of God.

19 - See the Angels

We go to see the angels,
In the House of Angels,
For we are lost and would be found.

To be lost is the Great Pain,
And the Great Sickness,
Relentless haunting,
Unquieting body and soul,
And we become afraid.

We come to the House of Angels,
To find our healing, our freedom,
From the slavery of the lost,
A bondage we did not wish for.

But it came anyway, upon us,
Every-carry burden,
Is a heavy weight,
Our backs are stooped,
When we come to the door,
Of the House of Angels.

Angels let us in,
They never refuse,
All are welcome,
I have a room,
In the House of Angels,
Where an angel comes,
And ministers me.

Many times it came out of me,
All the burden I carry,
Angel took it in hand,
And held it,
Took it off somewhere,
To bury it,
That is how I became restored.

After many a day,
I came to do the same,
I was shown how to do it,
It was my healing.

Now, as others come,
And knocked on the door,
I led them in,

And begin their healing,
In the House of Angels.

20 - Time's Touch

Death sat next to Life on a park-way bench,
Death spoke of his loss,
Life of her gain,
Until each said to the other,
"It is time's touch, my friend."

Together, each held out an arm,
With hands begging for alms,
That fell from Heaven.

Death said to Life,
"Enough of this my friend,
We have been around a long time,
Come let us unite ourselves together,
And become as one,
And greater shall we,
Than He,
Who is above."

Life said to Death,
"No my friend,
This cannot be so,
For all shall end,
If we join together,

And become nothing at all."

Death did not agree,
Even though he was aware it was true,
So he grabbed Life,
With arms wrapped all around
Her body,
And lo and behold,
They disappeared,
Down the Hole of Infinity.

This story has been told,
Now we are alone,
Since Infinity,
Has taken Death,
And Life away.

We are nowhere,
There is nothing,
To be somewhere,
To be someway,
Without Life and Death,
To show the way.

21 - The Alchemist Of Time

The Alchemist of time,
Is nudging the world a bit,
True time casts spells,
Of words,
Of the river,
We cross,
To get to the other side,
Of time and that river,
They are, we are,
Below the stars,
Of a moon-lost night,
We are lost,
That river and time are lost,
All, is lost,
All, is there to gain,
For we have none,
Time and that river,
Are gone,
Left us alone,
To gather our own,
Bits and pieces of time,
Left behind,

From the splashing,
Of the fallen moon,
Lost in that river and time.

22 - Walls of Fate

Walls of Fate,
Built by the architects of time,
Are massive,
And great,
Fortunate ones have come to celebrate,
This great wall,
Strengthened by stones of support,
That structure of the wise,
Foolishness in disguise,
Time with its materials,
Filled the day,
In an orderly way,
No gaps to be seen,
A perfection no one sees,
When there's no gap to be seen,
They have done their work well,
Lest the day be incomplete,
And our lives fall apart,
Like sometimes they do.
But today,
They are able and certain,
To accomplish their task,

So we can obtain,
That rich bounty,
Promised to us.

23 - Why Does the Lighthouse?

Why does the Lighthouse
Lose its light,
To the fog bound night,
That great absorber,
Of light and souls?

A House of Light,
Is very bright,
With its alliterations,
A genius of sorts,
It know its light's times,
For light and time,
Are interracially linked,
In their nature,
Sun-bound as they are,
By gravity,
That bends light and time,
On a course,
Set before eternity.

Mariner in a sea storm,
Close to crushing rocks,

Voyage of Odysseus,
Voyage of all sailors,
Whalers of the North Sea,
Vikings of iced lands,
Fishers on the Galilee,
Weathering a storm,
Calmed by the sleeping one,
The Lighthouse.

24 - Time and the Train
For The Grateful Dead

What is the time of train,
Riding in the train of time,
Headed for the Ever-Land Station,
Running its dreams on steam,
With an eye of elation?
A wonderful situation,
Terrapins dancing for the Queen.
What a wonderful scene.
End of the line,
We're just in time,
Pendants and balloons,
Under the strawberry moon,
Strung across from tree to tree,
What a sight to see,
Everyone here is free,
Fireflies dancing with you and me,
And the Terrapins for the Queen,
To the rhythm of dancing tambourine,
Its ribbons spinning in air,
Banjos playing everywhere.
Jerry Garcia was there,

Playing until dawn,
Singing every song,
Just like he did before,
He was dead and gone,
But not Bob Dylan or Ringo Starr,
They are still around,
That town,
Back there.
I hear the sound of time's train whistle,
Blowing,
"Last call, all on board!"
I must be going.
I shall not return here soon,
Not until the next,
Celebration of the Strawberry Moon.

25 - Creating Dragonflies

The Angel of the Shadows,
Is creating dragonflies again,
Each daintily drawn,
And painted with the heart of Michelangelo.

Michelangelo carved the Angel of Dragonflies,
Of finest marble stone,
Unlike any other of his angels hewn,
This one stood alone.

A statue's shadow,
Came alive,
And thrived in the stone garden,
And wanting color everywhere,
It dared to make a dragonfly,
Of iridescent hue,
And delight so,
To know,
Its beauty.

So it did again,
And again and again,

And still so now,
That is how,
Dragonflies,
Came to be.

26 - The Angel Craft

Neither angels nor demons,
Came to Obadiah's rescue,
From the Pit of Joseph.

It was the donkey of Balaam,
Seeing the Angels and Obadiah,
That dropped the rope,
And pulled him out.

Balaam's donkey gave a shout,
"Obadiah it that you?
I been searching all about,
We need you Obadiah,
For something is quite wrong,
All the angels are gone!
And God is angry!
Hurry, Obadiah, hurry along!"

Donkey showed Obadiah the way,
Through canyons of the desert,
To where he heard God say,
"Who scared my Angels away,

Who stole them, who broke them,
Who carried them away?
Even the demons are gone
My dark fallen ones!"

The robots came marching one by one,
See the Angels on the run,
Men of steel and iron cold,
Have no soul,
To be saved or lost,
There is no cost,
For them,
Robots do not die or feel pain,
Or get sick or injured in anyway,

The robots came marching two by two,
The demons did not know what to do,
Robots do not scare or burn in fire,
Don't lose their minds in mad desire,
Or hate, or kill,
It is not robots will,
Robots are peaceful,
Ever still.

The robots came marching three by three,
Robots have no need of the God of Trinity,
They are creatures of honest craft,
Who captured the Angels,
For the sake of Robot art,
Took them apart,
Cautiously crafting them back together again,
Made into something better,
Than Angels, Robots, God, and I.

27 - Trembling Moon

The trembling moon is lonely,
Knows its grief only,
Shows its grief with tears,
Where a bird's wing touches a cloud,
Deft movements of flight,
The wind is its friend.

To golden sand like grains of honey,
Droplets of the sun,
Are burning as they touch,
The beach and everyone.

A 9,000 year old Tree of Time,
Reaches its branches out,
Each one a timeline,
Of one lifetime,
Feathering out at its ends into green needles,
Fragrance of fir, cedar, and pine,
Near the ocean deep and green,
Where sovereign ships sail unseen,
By the Coquille river.

28 - Voice of the Hours

The counting clock has hands
And faces the feathered lands
Wing footed ferns seed the air,
Ghosts are there.
Ghosts of the air,
Being treasures of man,
In ancient candle-wood stands,
Of the dead sea,
Burn the shipwrecks of this world
Where I drink the milk of the moon.
And, no birds sing,
In the great mansions of the moon,
A haunted country,
Kingdom under the mere,
Vast chambers for the womb
Of treasuries are there
And sub-lunarian pools for fish.
Great fish engulf me there,
Like Jonah of old.
And I meet with fiddle and fable,
The dead stars that have become
Earth jewels like sacred scarabs

To protect and project our desires
I will not change my tears
For they are the fortunate ones
That fall to feed the flowers
And have the voice of the hours.

29 - Hands Gumble the Door

Hands gumble on the door
And feed the raging fire
Lighting the House of the Kingdom
That gives us shelter from ravens,
Ravens who dream of our lovely bones,
To pick and to peck,
When we are dead and alone.

But it was a strange clock
Whose time was read,
That told the ravens
When we were dead.

Now the raven picks my bones,
Pecks my bones,
For what is left of this dead poem.
Dead,
For everything has its season,
And its reason,
Then is gone.

30 - Fair Maid

What quest of day has come before her eyes?
Mist of her breath through forest rise.
The air is chill still in early morn.
Buttercups with dew lift their heads
To shed the night drop forms.
Elder oak of the forest
Came before her hazel eyes,
Her golden hair like sunlight fair,
And moved to tears,
She came near
The wise oak heart of the woods.
My wise heart
Became the Fool,
The Jester of the Woods.
I dance before all,
And play a tune on the Pipes of Pan,
Hoping to catch her if I can,
Fair Maid of the Forest,
Who stole my heart.
My heart knows God knows,
What love I have for thee
Fair Maid of the Forest.

Do not fear me,
This fool,
Come near,
For you are dear to me,
More precious you are to me,
Than all the diamond stars,
Jewel of my heart,
Fair Maid of the Forest.

31 - The Cruel War

Who kept the cruel war
Who killed the earth
It is something not so nice
If she wasn't so brave
Her life to save
She would be afraid
Still hidden in the night
But something clung to her heart
She loved without care
With the clover on the hills
The rabbit warrens of Dover
Waiting for all war to be over
Waiting for something kind
To be said
When the war was cruel
When the earth was dead
She lowers her head
Bows to the others
Among the clover
For the sake of a kind word,
She waits in silence.

32 - The Lonely Moon

I who wrote the World,
The role apples play in gravity,
Surprised the sea.
The glide of the moon,
Pulled the tide of the sea,
Further upon the beach,
Up the seaside cliffs,
It reaches,
Higher, seeking the nearer moon,
Which pulls it,
Tugs it,
Tries to capture it,
And make it its own,
To fill the empty mares,
Of the lonely moon.

33 - An Epithet for Delphi

Urge for the impossible
Surge of the tides
In the syntax of seaweed
Athens lies in ruins.
In the Archipelago of history
The invisible Church
Was well hidden
For time took meaning
Only in memory incorporating
The epithet for Delphi.

34 - Digital-to-Analog

Let us calculate the computational imagination
With my colored equations, my combinatorial art.
Speak to our new age of artificial intelligence
Of epoch dreams that break apart
And explore the genesis of the heart.
Cast your eyes away from guiding ideals and visions
Cast your eyes away you clockmakers, mechanics, and artisans,
Cast your eyes away from the digital promise
And find the analog life.

35 - The Shoreline

We spend our days
We spend our lives
Abiding
Life will contain
Silver time and rumors of the ruby ratio
Of days to flowers of antiquity
The waste and the want, do come not
To this foreign shore
Where the lighthouse has been lit
And the foghorn blows
Warning the waste and the want, not to come near,
For there is no antidote to this, I fear.

36 - Tablet Through Time

My, how your young computers have grown
Hammurabi, King of Babylon
Your code echoes in the old
Ready for something new
            a cultural narrative
A coral disposition in time
This disposition argues a cultivation
Beneath the sea
            having scores to settle with mankind.

37 - A Better Way

My God is kind,
Gentle of mind.
Not a God of apocalypse,
Not a God of hard tests,
Floods and blood.
There is a better way to teach
Each and every one.
By example my God does it,
Just as mother to each son and daughter,
Just as father to every sister and brother.

38 - The Avenue

Down the Avenue of the homeless heart,
An old man said, "Don't grow too quick my child, for that means I'll
be gone soon.
And I, still love to dance with you,
under the harvest moon."

Down the Avenue of the homeless heart,
The street lamps lit one by one,
The cats came out and pawed about for mice on the run, curiosity on
the prowl,
with night cat's meow.

Down the Avenue of the homeless heart,
In the cold, in the dark-way, quiet, hidden in an alley,
I lay to sleep, my soul to keep, I'm hungry, so cold and hungry, I shake,
I fall asleep,
and do not wake.

39 - Unity

The poet broke the walls
Not the trumpet's call.
Powerful poet
Paints the Angels he saw,
The authority given to him
By the Angels of the Fall.
"We are One," this poet calls,
Then the Angels come,
For the poet and the Angels are One.

40 - Purposing the Wind

We rise to see the newborn wind,
Purposing it to touch the angels.
Spirals of wing,
Brambles of air,
Caught our attention,
Bursting into a million eddies.
Currents of the wind
At our command
Effort the breeze
With limitless seeds
Of bursting pressure,
Exploding into nano-stars
Too tiny to be seen
Except by the angels,
Who see everything under the sun.
For all, is under their watch,
Given to them by God.
Golden and glistening are nano-star droplets
Before the faces of angels.
It is the kind heart of the wind
We have obtained,
It will have to be enough.

41 - My Shadow Angels

My shadow angels
Fail at night
When there is no light
To cast them.

Just before this is so,
I let them go
To run
And find the sun.

For my shadow angels,
Savior, is the day,
When all wonders of the world
Are lit up for display.

Complications
We lay upon the children
Are too much for angels to bear.

It is the worst hurt
The most unkind
Causing anguish

In a young child's mind.

Do not get caught
Being uninvited intentions
Of complex complications
That even you do not understand.

I cannot let this go on any more,
So I'm telling you,
All the angels of my shadows.

42 - A Pine-ary Logic of Trees

A pine-ary logic of trees
Counts the greenery.
All the blades of grass
Are sharp for the cutting.
In battle they shall wound,
Star-touched children,
Gift of the wind's hour.

In the heartless woods,
Hear dark raven's sins.

Naked stars
Are the morning-kin's hope
Of something greater,
As she lays her eggs on the sun.

Airfields are ripe for the harvest.
Winged reapers are air-cleared into land.
Begin the reaping
Of bounty of the mane
Of airfields.
Clouds are there too.

Clouds for the witness of the harvest,
For angels are no more.
I am saddened.
I go to find out what happened to them.
For I need the angels.
You do too.

43 - Beyond Imagination

Curious flora,
Time travels the dawn
Enchanting the forest and fawn,
When the sun has come along.

In rare triumph,
Beyond imagination,
Enlist the sun,
For its moment has come.

Still centuries ahead,
Is the garden
Bringing the world
Into its own,
And needed,
If it is to go on,
Revolutionizing the binomial pauses,
And hand colored poems,
For something better than the churches.

What they know isn't working,
Like it's supposed to do,

The kingdom of God isn't found there,
It is written in my poems.

44 - King of the Lost Poets

For Abramatlot, King of the Lost Poets,
Time is a book of prayers of a sacred sun.
Birds ride, tied to the golden one.
Out of morning new sounds come,
And a light of a new kind.
There is magic for the landing place of the griffins,
Near the flowers of the hippogriff.
Morning glittered down on the world,
Abramatlot gave a cry,
Ran down the swooped way.
Nests of dawn-light glazed his world
That only the sad saw through trees.
A dawn-light kiss surrenders to it,
Where the thousand nights
Of the blazing moon
Are set for the King of the Lost Poets' adventure.

45 - This House of Poems

This house of poems
Is my shelter of a kind
And brave are the walls
Of foundations rhyme
Time is set in its stones
But I alone
Would roam
From my sheltered place
And grab the tempest by the tail
And ride the racing tide

Tides of time
Deposit sediments of my rhymes
Layered over the years
Carved by a river into a new canyon
It did flow with living waters.

And the world watched
My ribbon flow of words.
They did not know what they heard,
Did not know what to do
And make of it all.

They thought me a curious find,
Not of their kind,
And strange in all I was,
To be suspected, rejected,
Tested beyond all tested.
I did my best
To pass the test
But it may just take time
To cure them all.
So I crawl
Back to my home of poems,
Where the sun of winter has no friends.
The graveyard told him so.

46 - Beam of the Sun

With a structured beam of the sun,
I stand alone
Having spoken my last poem,
Knowing love is a heart broken
And a light spoken.

Its seeds have been planted,
Near the altar of the last child born.
I slept to cross the border of time
And enter the realm of the beggar's hunger
Where roots in the earth are strong and deep
And the sun of another country rose.
In my empty cup, I caught the tear of an angel,
Let loose my pen-dragon,
The beast of the gravestone rose to meet it
Then there was a cloud.

Cloud child,
Where did you go?
For the wind has come up,
I need to know.
I looked up to the sky

Nowhere did I spy
Where the cloud child
Did go.

47 - Dust Bowl Pirates

Dust bowl pirates
Listen to the stars.
A light-clock shines there
And lightning bolts for Mars.

The frog that loves the library
Croaks what he reads at night,
To listening stars and fireflies,
To the dust bowl pirates' delight,
The notes of his throat
Croaks the words to be heard.

This is what he reads:
"You will never know,
Where you are going to go,
For going to go,
Is nowhere to go,
So go and get going,
To get the knowing,
Where to get going to go."

48 - Walk Away From the Apocalypse

Come with me! Come with me!
And see
This new heaven.
Oh! I have made it with my stars
And angel feathers given
Upon,
The day of redemption
We do not need it!

For, I have conceived it,
This new heaven,
And I will take you there
With tenderness and care
Upon my back.
Oh! Come with me I insist,
And walk away from the apocalypse.

49 - Clocks' Cascade

And I, caught flight,
With the feathers of arrow in quiver,
Across the ever-river,
Of clocks' cascade.
Clever are the stars below.

Earth-stars there are,
To be eaten by glowing worms.
They are our thoughts,
Whose strong bones survive
Sudden shifts of the sun,
Sudden shafts of the sun,
Their deluge.

And it burns in the heart and hall of home.
I came to the never-naming of my soul.
My true name is in this poem.

50 - Constantine the Rabbit

Constantine the Rabbit lives
With glitters of gold
Shining out one last season
Of impeccable reason
Before time broke the earth,
With invaders from two worlds.

The Neep is very happy
To see Constatine at play,
With Rumi the instigator
Of commentary croons,
With typewriter rhythm
Tapping words on the moon.

Undone was his marvelous mask.
I saw at last,
The lost face of Rumi.

51 - Oh, Angel

Oh, angel of the impossible wing,
It is you I hail
For I propose,
A death interrupted,
There is something I need to say.

Oh, angel of death,
Take a breath,
Rest awhile,
For, I need, a death interrupted
And time enough to tell.

Oh, angel of my breath
It is your words I quest,
For, I need, a death interrupted,
Time enough to tell them,
How much I care for them.

Oh, angel of my care,
Fly everywhere
Across the stillborn sky
To seed my words upon the earth

Until it is time to die
And no more be, a death interrupted.

52 - Where the Sleek Clock Coils Its Time Tightly

Cormorants in caves
By the sea-dipped sand,
And sun grains upon the sea,
Come, celebrate the day with me.

Fishers Keep
By fisheries deep,
And treasures under the sea,
Come, share the treasure with me.

Minnows who swim in rivers cold,
All the wonders you behold,
And swim to the crooked sea,
Come, share your wonders with me.

Where we weep for tomorrow's fallen stars,
Swept away Mercury and Mars,
And far into the celestial sea,
Come, adventure there with me.

Where the sleek clock coils its time tightly.

53 - Harper the Angel

Pretend this day dream, this day scheme,
For Harper the Angel did strum
A tune for bells to be rung.
For the essence of things
The bells did ring.

No angel hood
Covered Harper's face
Lest Harper be misunderstood
About the case of race
An angel has no race.

Harper is a special case
This angel is a race,
Of one.
Vibrating synergy,
Son
Of eternity
Did dwell
In heaven
Quail
Did run to ride the hill's crest
Wings tucked to side,
And Harper the Angel was there.

54 - Specimens of Dawn

Specimens of dawn
A river forgotten runs
To the lost sea of Babylon

Time consumed path
Falls behind me
Leaving only future's way
Left before me

Tease or test
My ship clock
Is at the dock
Time for me to go
Then no time at all
For me to be
Say the waves of the Babylon Sea.

55 - Adversarial Pixels

Adversarial pixels and binaries
Are Time's test
Of the People of the Red Willow River
Only they could cast a scared shadow
And holy are their fears.

Unjust mistrusts invaded their vast valley
And winds gather there
For, from far, all the winds have come
Singing holy songs,
And forever are their years.

The Red Velvet Valley has seen
The Red Willow River's dream
Of water even flow and pure
From angels cry above,
For many are their tears.

56 - A Prophetic Word

A prophetic word
Once again heard
Like feathers on the fly
Or whispers on the wind
They are nothing
In the weather vane of the vain
But again they do claim it is so
Of some important meaning to know
They wish it so
But it is not God's intent
It is just the wind He does send
And angels ten
To show the truth
To the one who sat quietly under the sun
Writing poems that show the bright new day.

57 - In the Places

In the places of our dreams,
Connection and acceptance
Are waving at the Universe.

Our memories deem it so,
So we can know what is important to know
In our soul,
And keep it there,
And be aware of it,
Where the mountains touch the universe
Frozen in one forever moment.

Movement of time suspended
Then contended to begin again.

After its rest,
The clock talked
Telling tales
With rhythm in its geared bones.

Stones of time break apart
And become sand upon the eternal beach,

Where I reach to the teaching stars.

As long as one and one are two
I shall be here for you.

58 - Angel of Time

Who is this angel of time
I have come to know
Like a paradox flower
That in the garden did grow?

A nested bird below
Where a terrapin crawled too slow
In the sand of time.

Word of life in healing hand,
And butterfly friend upon the land
Of the angel band,
And this angel of time,
Is a friend of mine.

59 - The Clock

The clock stopped its tock.
Its analog tick
Gave a digital twist to its name.
I saw its flame burning.
A shadow rested there for a while, not moving.
Then time began again with dancing flame,
Set my heart yearning
For all hours that are done
And all the hours yet to come
That shall be gone too soon,
Chasing the racing moon.

60 - Who

Who, like my neighbor, God,
With the amethyst of liberty,
Beneath the tree and thorny crown,
Little angels did abound,
With proud apparition,
And soft sun sound.

There is a flower nearer to thee,
And heaven's possibilities.
I am bound to the earth,
A lost world with another day
To steal away my soul's liberty,
If I allow it,
Where I see the possibilities
Written in the heavens,
Near the starry seas.

61 - Once an Angel

Once there was an angel
Who walked a thousand miles to church.
When the angel got there,
Nobody cared,
For the angel wasn't what they expected.

62 - Angels Came to Rest

When the angels came to rest...
Seventeen angels and seventeen demons,
At my table did attest,
I count them as even,
Seventeen parables I feed them,
Like the seventeen bells of heaven,
I hoped to set them free,
From God's slavery.

63 - When Time Stopped

When time stopped,
There was no life left,
For the poet of the clock,
When miles apart,
We did sing,
Of the poet, the clock,
And the feathery King.

And if the feathered bird should fly,
Above us so far and high,
That we shall all see,
And sing of it with glee,
Of something so fine and free,
Before we are gone forever.

64 - Thirty-Four Colors

Thirty-four colors,
Seventeen for angels,
Seventeen for devils,
I pondered what this could mean.
Shall the bells toll for me?
Shall I find the sanctuary,
From the broken sea,
Broken by seventeen angels,
And seventeen devils?
The flood comes to me,
The rainbows fall,
Thirty-four colors for it all.

65 - Seventeen Angels

Seventeen angels stood,
Before the fountains of time,
Upon Endeavor Mountain,
They are friends of mine.
Quiet they were,
All hushed in their breath.
I came there, upon my death.

Though the breezes were cold,
With north wind bold,
The fountains of the mountain
Shot high before my contentious eye
Upward ever still,
And shadows of seventeen angels stood still
Before the fountains of time.
Ghosts and empty shells of friends of mine
They were.
I puzzled this in my death
Alone, forever, in my last rest.

66 - The Secret of Time

The secret of time,
Is the halo of angels,
For light is time's expression,
God's extension,
Photon's definition.

There is a light that shines from within,
Without its beginning,
For halos of angels are there,
And do abound,
One for each of us,
I have found.

67 - The World Doesn't End

Today, the world doesn't end,
Though some may wish it to,
It seems a terrible world to them,
So they would prefer to see it end.

But not today, for you see,
It is needed by me,
And some friends,
For a time, yet.

The golden fields of harp strings,
We shall reap before we sleep,
For angel harps gold and white.

68 - Worship Is Ours

But worship is ours
And the angels
For His divinity
Is what we see in our hearts
Lit by the Father of lights
And the Son of light
It is our delight!

69 - Morning Worship

The light has come
Music for the Lord
In heaven above
Where the angels sing
To the glory of our King

70 - Worship of Fire

Worship of fire,
Spirit of light,
Word of wonder,
Manger child delight,
Star filled night
Was there,
And Angels everywhere.
"Do not be afraid!
For we bring tidings of great joy."
A little baby boy is born
Where wise men three
Came to see the sight
Following a wandering star
To that wondrous night.

71 - At Water's Edge

At water's edge,
The Bell of Dawn
Tolls the morning again,
With Birds of Avalon
At rest in the night,
Soon to take flight,
To where angels are in light.

And when the hills grow old,
And the wind blows cold,
They fly to the Sanctuary of the Sun,
The Providence of the Moon,
Persistent,
For the Shadow is to pass soon,
Where angels are in light,
And my Sanctuary Dreams are true.

72 - First Love

First love,
Enter a life
Remembered as a season,
Enchantment under the trees,
Witchcraft and geometries,
Pentacles of time,
In a comet of my mind.

How intense sentiments and emotions,
Such explosions,
That struggle to fathom a series of photon impulses,
Light of our love will endure,
Dawning forever, to name my longing.

This wayward heart has come again,
Into that heated summer,
Oasis for the soul,
Awaken this garden troll.
Yet my heart is not stone,
I love with all my might.

73 - Is the Wind?

Is the wind the color of the sky
or is it separate of another sight
can it be decreed in colors so bright
or in the darkness of the night
or in a burning star, so far?

The forest and the flower
want to know
a notion of trans-sensory,
electric, aglow,
where the little giants go
to see the colors of time.

74 - Love, Lonely

Love, lonely, the past and the future
if vacant you are
meaning, lover of wisdom
so I'm told
of revolution bold,
the poet stands for life.

Amid mechanical strife
of mean machines
and broken bone,
the poet stands for life.

With thematic mechanics
with tools for a poem
landscapes of possibilities
mystic chants of human soul
it is just my poem
and nothing more,
the poet stands for life.

75 - The Hardest Things

The hardest things:
So few the grains of happiness
So Dark the scales of balance
In weighing the world
How a blink by nothingness
Did make a universe
For black is the hole of nothingness
That returns again each time
For each time is due
Radiating from the pages
Of forgotten love letters home.

Relish the optional mind
In consonance and carry-ness
Alone,
Glitter in the sky
Find your way home.

76 - Inverse, Out-verse

Inverse, out-verse
Godmother of the soul
Her perfect love has no fear
Mother of one and all
Mary, Martha
Love of Jesus
Come before us
We bow at the feet of Jesus
Come one, come all
To the fount of every blessing
With the Angels Before the Throne.

77 - Heart-lux

Heart-lux, light of love
Clock-lux, tap of time
Word-lux, make a rhyme
Machine-lux, geared crime
Free-flux, flowing mind
Poetic heart, poetic kind
Heart to share, friend of mine.

78 - Tinker With Time

Different size gears
an intricate system
for measuring time
and calculation.

Construct a whole architecture
rendering the possible
generating inventions
into more simple elements
of mystical thinkers
who tinker with time.

79 - An Angel With a Pendulum Bell

An angel with a pendulum bell
Came to my clock
I knew so well
Came to talk of its tick and its tock
And how it would beat and how it would not
And when it would be silent
Waiting for the call
Of bells to ring
Choir to sing
In my heart's bright sun.

80 - Past and Future

Past and future do not exist
only our memory does
only the present exists
and future changes go unknown
and future challenges are unknown
the effect of the past is a mystery
we cannot tell what is future
and what is history
when one ends
and the other begins,
neither last.

In the end
each moment of the future
becomes the past
in the newer present.

That is its essence
that is all there is,
the ever, newer present.

81 - One Hour

One hour to witness
One to testify
One to consider
One to touch the sky
One to take the dare
One to just not care
One to walk away
One to be there for a day
One hour to watch
One to waste away
One hour to hate
One hour to love
All the hours are from heaven above...

All the hours are free for me
To take and to choose
Which hour will it be?

82 - Nothing

Nothing the zero
More meaningful
Than I can know
That nothing
Can impact everything
Is a mystery
I must know
In a primitive sense
Zero has more meaning
Than infinity
Lacking a value
It is valuable to me
This empty place
This empty space
With respect to keeping time
In my time-jar.

83 - Something Speaks

Something speaks to us in our sleep
Something seeks us in our dreams
And if there is a counterpoint to all of this
It is not as it seems
For point and counterpoint
Anoint the compass of time
And if we should sleep our lives away
And if we should dream our dreams away
To somewhere far
It is okay
For such dreams there are.

84 - To the Holy People, Most High

To Become the Wisdom of God,
A Holy People
Shall be one,
For all the Earth is Mine.

The Righteousness and the Redemption,
The Sanctification and the Passion,
Is from Him...
Touch the soul
With the empathy of music,
Sing His Angels above,
Guardians of His love.
Play a Passion tune,
Sing the Sun and the Moon,
The greater for the day,
The lesser for the night,
Set your heart's delight,
On Him.

85 - Ode to Someone's...

Pure presence, my friends,
There's no such thing as separation.
All we are are circles about a star,
Circles around the sun,
Each and every one
Bright and shining,
Even if we don't know it,
Don't show it,
Sometimes, for a while.
Are you another god my loves,
Are you all angels from above,
Who circles about my star?
Oh, I see your light from far.
Come close to to my orbit, my loves,
Come close to my star, everyone.

86 - Once an Angel

Once there was an angel
Who came to earth
Disguised as a poet
(You all just don't know it)
For the purpose of revelation
Of a new kind
In the shadow of the Tower of the Devil
In Montana,
Close Encounters of an Angelic Kind.

87 - Sounds of the Future

I hear the sounds of the future
Where my memory is already written
I just haven't got there yet
But I hear it in the far.

I am large enough to know this
Small enough to care
For if my memory shall survive me
It will get me there.

Every instant, once a giver,
Once a taker,
It will take me there,
For the future is made
Of every instant
And just a little bit more.

88 - Called the Dead

Called the dead and gone
They cross the endless rift,
Gap of eternity, bottomless well,
Infinite barrier, of no time
For all time to come.

The living shall not reach them
Until they are gone as well
Let the living live for a little while,
Each life has its time to tell
Of itself and I would hear
Each and every one before
They and I are gone.

89 - What Beckons Us

What beckons us
To the mountain
To the sea
You and I
To fall in love with a time
We shall yet perceive,
And explore it with great subtlety and profundity
Disguised as a poem
What we have known
For two-hundred years.
The tower clock yet tolls
In downward arc.
A child shall know
What it is time will tell,
The wish
Found in the wishing well.
I do wish to know
Where I shall go
When I die,
I wish to know,
For the unknown of death
Scares me so.

90 - What Is This New Star

What is this new star we see?
A wandering Star in the East,
We come to worship Thee
Traveling far from the West,
Where the North Wind blows
Across the Southern Sea.
We come with gifts for Thee.
We come Kings, one, two, and three.

An infant child we found,
With shepherds there around,
To see the Lamb of God
Born under the Star of Bethlehem
In the Night of Israel.
A Word, a Light,
And Angels in that night.
"Do not fear, we bring near,
Good tidings of great joy
A gift,
A baby boy
Is given to you."

And that was long ago,
Yet this I still know,
I see that Star of Wonder,
I see that Word of Light,
In the night,
In the day,
A gift was given to me,
And I, King of Little Angels,
Have received it unto me.
It is there ever still,
And shall always be.

91 - Time Is a Wonderful Poet

Time is a wonderful poet.
The papayas, persimmons,
And poppies know it.
Though the gomphothere is gone
Its time is lost,
At the cost of evolution
And yet the ground sloth lives.
Life exists that doesn't fit
The scheme of times present theme
It is the poetic justice of life's dreams.

92 - White Bloom

White bloom
Frail and brief,
Quiet is my heart
By the sea.
Who has seen us there,
Thou and me,
My apple tree blossom?
Quick, so they should know, I vow
My love, trouble, sticks and stones
Bone of bones, and a marble cross
In the garden spot.
Wiser am I to know,
To gather not the dew.
To cross the street, to see the light
By your window, cost me nothing,
But loses me everything I call love.
Ride the dories on the river of the sun,
When I am done and the sands run out,
And the hour glass is empty.
It is gravity that has stolen my time away.

93 - When We Dream

When we dream,
The shadows are darkest,
The parables are hardest,
And most essential for the harvest
Of mankind.
Even the sovereignty is there
To unravel the world,
That churning mechanism
That is the visionary clock
That sees all time in an instant and forever
Just like in that other poem of mine
Written earlier,
Meditative parallels upon the fair world
Of hobos in the city.

94 - The Exo-Gram

The exo-gram came
On it, it had my name
Nietzsche saw it in his dream
You know the one I mean,
The one with the golden time machine.

95 - The Gargoyles Dream

The gargoyles dream,
Of a soul friend
To awaken his flesh
From stone
To free his soul
To let the universe know
I am here
Like art, like life,
I am here.
Do not deny that I am real
And feel just like you do,
For there is a universe teeming with life,
For there is a gargoyle set in stone in the night
To watch above the cathedral
For the lost saints of time.

96 - Poet Cosmologist

Poet cosmologist,
Apologist, for Apollo,
Cosmic conjurer,
Prism ponderer,
Monumental moment,
Gazing glimpse,
Time's twist,
Elements exist,
The universe is in this poem.

97 - Buddha Breath

Buddha breath,
Googolnaught
Where is the burial plot
For, the Queen of American Spiritualism
Of the golden narrative
Of the hypothesis of God?
A latter-day pandemic has come
And stolen the sun
For the extinction of that brave light,
Of light and time,
That friend of mine.

98 - Meadow of Time

And in this meadow of time,
The magic number you hide.
Four forces of nature are tied together
In this mathematical magpie magi,
Of the moonlit meadow,
And sundial shadow.
Hide the clocks of your heart
In this meadow of time.

99 - Collage of Light

Life is a collage of light
And shadows lost in the night
Where the lightning strikes
A beat to love affairs
In letters to light
And illuminate the darkness
Briefly
I read the words written across the sky
"It is not for thee I die,
But for the butterfly."

Where love is lost,
And the tempest heart is shaken,
That looks upon my love,

To every star, a start,
And time, a fool is not,
But an error of my compass heart,

Yet time,
Bends with wind-driven sun,
With brief hours,

Time's fool, at the edge of flowers,
Is my love,

Then comes my heart, a kiss
To your rosy cheeks and lips.

100 - Lobadoodle

Lobadoodle,
Robot-whisperer,
Your life is in a tohubohu.
Behold the wonder of its chaos
Extending across the universe
And back again to home
Through the transcendent boundaries of time.

Richard Lee Granvold, born in 1952, has written poetry since 1966. He has filled many roles in life—from toy store clerk to A.I. researcher, United States Army soldier to mathematician—and these experiences have shaped his poetic expressions. Native Oregonian by birth, Granvold is now retired and living in Albany, Oregon, where he writes poetry, novels, and plays mandolin while enjoying life with his wife, daughter, and grandchildren.

CPSIA information can be obtained
at www.ICGtesting.com
Printed in the USA
FSHW021851210421
80630FS

9 781736 314821